English cathedrals and the visual arts:
patronage, policies and provision 2005

English cathedrals and the visual arts: patronage, policies and provision 2005

Tom Devonshire Jones & Graham Howes

Art & Christianity Enquiry

A+
CE

Published by Art & Christianity Enquiry
107 Crundale Avenue, London NW9 9PS
T & F +44 (0)20 8206 2253
enquiries@acetrust.org
www.acetrust.org

ISBN 0-9551485-0-2

Contents

Introduction

The preparation of this book has cause, occasion and purpose. The community of the Church provided the cause and the world of art the occasion; its purpose is to bring the two together, and to address them in terms of equal love. One should say bring the two together again, for the centuries in which both conversed are numerous if distant, and today's re-engagement is fragile and of recent origin, a mere five minutes in the long day of church history. In what follows, therefore, present and future need considering within tradition's long process.

In the last fifteen years or so the Churches can be said to have rediscovered art, a period in which the place of art in British life – in its culture, economy and higher education – began to loom large. In the ecclesiastical sphere there had been false dawns – the 1940's commissions at St Matthew Northampton to Moore and Sutherland, and Coventry Cathedral and the purchase of the Methodist Collection of Modern Religious Art in the 1960s. It is only very recently, however, that cathedrals and artists now freely approach one another to discuss exhibitions and commissions; that residencies (following Durham's initiative of 1984) of varying duration have been set up in cathedrals, churches and colleges; that teaching and preaching have reached out to appropriate the complex art factor in Christianity. Recognising this complexity, many have taken refuge in icons, sensing here a safe and hallowed solution, an endpoint to art in church life, at the very time when fresh, forward looking engagement is called for.

We were not aware of any survey of these recent developments, whose energy, often with high profile in the media, merited study. The Anglican cathedrals have proved a fascinating group, located as they are all over England.

The occasion of our study arose from the puzzlement of a senior Visual Arts Officer of Arts Council England who was finding Cathedral Chapters and Committees' applications, quite apart from their theological categories, somewhat arcane. Hence our questionnaire and its analysis, and the reflections on the process of the artwork itself. These chapters are set against the work of the statutory bodies entrusted with the care of cathedrals and churches. These functions are listed in the Appendix. To those who question the need for such bodies it must be answered that Christianity has never been blind to the power of the visual arts: it would not take the trouble it does were it not for the high hopes it has of artists in its work of worship and service and teaching. Artists who complain of a church committee's critical attitudes are often underestimating the potency that art has placed in their hands.

The purpose, therefore, of our enquiry has been to acquaint artists and church people with our findings, and to draw both in on the present situation as we have found it. Too often commissions have disappointed and exhibitions failed for want of understanding and proper preparation. Art as commodity quickly becomes marginal, to the loss and impoverishment of both artist and church. Against this background of not infrequent failure the four case studies provided by Mark Cazalet (in a way that we as cleric and academic knew we could not) bring into this book the tang of creativity's rhythm and risk. We believe that a step-by-step and 'How To' text put into the hands of a church member, cleric or churchwarden contemplating a commission or wishing to welcome an exhibitor may well lead to a tired, lifeless outcome. The world of art is best approached by going where the artists are, and engaging once more in the conversation of art with religion. In such an encounter each has everything to gain.

Last, it is a pleasure to recall and record thje numerous occassions we have had cause for gratitude to the Dean and Chapter in mant cities, to artists, and to Arts Council England and the Jerusalem Trust, without whose help our work would not have been accomplished.

1

The questionnaire: analysis of data

Introduction

A preliminary questionnaire (see Appendix 1) was sent – in May 2002 – to the 43 Deans of Church of England Cathedrals, with Gibraltar also included. Forty-one replies were received by 31 August. Although they varied greatly in the degree of detail supplied, the variety of policies and practices described, and in the quality of theological reflection involved, the aggregate data presented below suggest some relatively significant configurations. These are set out in the order of the questionnaire itself, although the small number of respondents (the response rate itself, however, was very high) and the relatively 'open-ended' nature of the questions posed made sophisticated statistical inference virtually impossible.

Section A Theological and pastoral

A1 *How would you describe your Chapter's main motives for commissioning and/or exhibiting works of art in a Cathedral setting, especially in relation to (a) Worship (b) Doctrine (c) Mission?*

Here Worship was mentioned by 28 respondents. Sometimes works of art were deemed 'to add another dimension to worship in addition to words and music', 'to stimulate the imagination in its response to facts', to 'develop Christian spirituality' and 'convey a sense of calm and wonder, privacy and community'.

Almost the same number of respondents (27) placed equal emphasis upon Mission, sometimes 'to attract, engage and perhaps outrage the visitor' more often as a means to 'convey profound and timeless truth in an imaginative yet contemporary way', and as a direct adjunct to Mission itself, when 'the visitor's aesthetic and imaginative response to a work of art can be the first stage of the evangelization of that person'.

In contrast rather fewer respondents (21) opted for an overtly Doctrinal context for works of art. Sometimes 'churchmanship' was invoked (eg 'now conservative orthodox') or blanket statements ('to express the doctrine we know') provided. Occasionally a more profound theology was articulated where, as one respondent put it, 'the Word was not made flesh in order to be turned back into Word again. Art can help incarnate the Word of God,' or where, for example, Mark Cazalet's work was seen as 'setting the values of relationships, sacrifice and freedom within the context of the present day'. It is worth noting, however, that seven respondents saw the relationship of worship, doctrine and mission as essentially integral, even if analytically separable. As one put it, their Chapter's main motives for placing art in a cathedral setting were 'to enhance the beauty of the building in a contemporary idiom, and to stimulate thought, questioning and dialogue about the Christian faith'.

A2 *If you have remained inactive in this area, please indicate any primary constraints operative in your case.*

Here a significant number of respondents (28) regarded the question as inapplicable to them as they were indeed active in varying degrees. While specific constraints were occasionally cited (eg 'the apathy of Chapter and clergy' and 'CFCE (see page 57) ambivalence towards art projects') and one respondent spoke bluntly of 'other priorities here', nearly a quarter of respondents (10) regarded finance as their primary constraint. 'We do very little commissioning', wrote one, 'because financial margins are very tight.' 'Lack of funds' said another.

These responses can be related to those given to question B7 (*In your own case were the primary constraints on commissioning architectural, liturgical or financial [please be as specific as you can]*)? where 21 respondents placed finance ('we would love be in a position to commission more', 'we have no money'. 'By the time the design was available to us the financial climate had changed and the project was proving hard to progress') before architectural (15) or liturgical (6) considerations. (Responses are analysed in detail under B7 below.)

A3 *How seriously does your Chapter take the relationship between religion, artworks, beliefs and experience in your own 'public space' among (a) congregations and (b) visitors.*

Although one respondent appeared not to understand our question ('what do you mean?') and another replied 'Don't know', nine took the relationship 'seriously' and – more significantly – 20 voluntarily upped their answer to 'very seriously indeed'. Among both groups combined (*ie* 29) the majority (14) made no formal distinction between visitors and congregation, seeing artworks as 'matter for dialogue with both' or as enabling 'a proper response from both the congregation and visitors' . One respondent saw art and music as helping 'to make present the musicians. This applied equally to congregations' stating eloquently that 'a holistic approach is essential. The visitor and the regular worshipper should both find a harmony in the different elements of the space, experiencing it as sacred space as well as public space'. Others took a less holistic stance. Three made a distinction between the needs of (a) and of (b). One told us how 'instruction about art and art history is offered to the congregation and careful signage and presentation is important for visitors' while another was clear that 'for the congregation, modern liturgies can benefit from modern objects used in the liturgy. For visitors modern artwork can be a way of drawing less committed believers to the building and giving something they can respond to'. Three other respondents were even more focussed. One saw their arts programme as eventually 'a continuing and important part of the Chapter's own life together and of our ministry', another as the means whereby 'the Chapter and community is being led to perceive the importance of non-verbal communication', while a third confessed frankly that 'although we wish to make as full use as we can of the visual arts to enhance our worship and liturgy, our chief concern in our commissions and exhibitions is to address the needs and aspirations of our visitors. Many of our most important recent commissions....are not in the main worship space and are out of sight of our worshipping congregation'.

Our question also elicited some less enthusiastic responses (7) most of which reported a broadly lukewarm stance ('we all see 'value' but I wouldn't say we are passionate'). One remarked that 'with the pressure of work on the Chapter, only two of us full time, this is an unrealistic question' and two more hinted that division within the Chapter itself limited initiatives ('several members of the Chapter would take this relationship very seriously, but corporately we have not given a great deal of time to it'). However, responses *in toto* indicate a very high level of serious consideration being given by many Chapters to the relationship between religion, artworks, beliefs and experiences.

A4 *How do you encourage the personal input of the artist(s) involved?*

This question, which links strongly to B4 and B6 below, revealed a highly variegated relationship with the artists involved. Although some degree of Chapter involvement was a common denominator for 16 respondents, its precise nature ranged from an explicitly 'hands-off' approach ('they are not artisans – they are artists and we therefore seek their creative input and give only general guidelines') to relatively moderate Chapter input ('a free hand after a fairly tight brief') to such formalized procedures as 'a competition', 'getting them to write about their work which we then reproduce in leaflets' or 'each artist/craftsman, following the guidance of Chapter and Architect, outlines their intentions in a drawing which can then be discussed, amended, etc.' This latter procedure was not seen as necessarily fail-safe. In one case 'the initial procedure was discussed with Chapter, FAC and at an open meeting. It received a mixed reception, and is currently 'on the back burner'', and in another it was felt more important for artists 'particularly to experience a cross-section of Cathedral liturgies and other events in order to resource and ground them in our life and mission'. But overall most respondents (19) cited 'discussion', 'ongoing dialogue', 'extended conversation with the artist' as integral to the process of encouragement, and terms like 'identify', 'working partnership', 'letting them into our processes of thinking' and 'building mutual trust' recurred regularly among the replies to this question. Overwhelmingly (12) the initiative for this appeared to come from a collective Chapter decision, although not infrequently from individuals. Chapter members (7) with specific 'knowledge and expertise and contacts' were deemed critical in developing a personal relationship with the artist in question. In one instance, a Dean appeared to act without reference to his Chapter (who 'show very little interest, they leave it to me') in involving a particular artist. In another, conversely, the artist was 'encouraged to visit, and perhaps even 'man' the exhibition, but we [*ie* the Chapter] have had only little involvement'.

Section B The process of patronage

B1 *What, if any have been the sources of patronage for the visual arts in your cathedral, whether (a) permanent works of art or (b) temporary exhibitions?*

Analysis of this question revealed some interesting configurations. Although seven Chapters drew solely on their own existing resources (sometimes including recent benefactions) and another 17 considered their 'Friends' as a primary resource – sometimes (7) indeed as the only source of patronage – there was firm evidence of even stronger dependence on private and corporate donations (20) ranging from single benefactions and bequests to Yorkshire Water and, in two instances, the Freemasons. Temporary exhibitions were, in turn, heavily dependent (9) upon local and regional government support and upon regional arts associations. Almost as strong (14) was the use of major grant giving bodies eg Heritage Lottery (3), European Fund (1) and the Pilgrim Trust (1) and established charitable trusts at national (eg the Jerusalem Trust) and at local levels. What is clear is that to date, on this evidence, the sourcing of patronage by Chapters appears to be a relatively unsystematic and eclectic procedure, and that in the most successful if not necessarily the most resourceful strategies (evident in six identifiable cases) patronage has been sought simultaneously within and beyond the Cathedral community and also from charitable trusts and private benefactors.

B2 The broad picture established here (*Has patronage been primarily ecclesiastical or lay?*) showed, fairly predictably, that lay patronage (22) which included Friends of Cathedrals as well as private benefactors was more prominent than ecclesiastical patronage (9) which was primarily from the Chapter itself. A further eight respondents defined their patronage base as both ecclesiastical and lay.

Five other respondents regarded available patronage as either problematic ('reactive and opportunistic'), moribund ('it is some years since a permanent work of art was commissioned in the Cathedral') or non-existent ('we are too poor').

B3 *What forms might such sources of patronage take in future?*

In responses received to this question the pattern revealed above is already anticipated. Ten respondents foresaw a more 'mixed economy' approach as a prerequisite for success (as opposed to the six who reported having actually done so under question B2) and several others (4) who predicted more approaches to 'external bodies' to 'trust funding as well as existing resources' and 'as financial margins get tighter, individual patrons may become more important'. Some more specific innovations were anticipated – 'more temporary exhibitions,' a role for 'our new Development Officer in seeking patronage for the arts' and in one case 'the creation of formal partnerships between eg local Universities, Colleges, Art Galleries, etc and the Cathedral'. Most respondents (26), however, chose to predict a similar pattern of patronage as at present, while three others remained 'unsure', and the remainder (11) chose not to answer the question at all. One lone, bullish voice, nonetheless, sounded a contrary, optimistic note 'we would like to think that, as the nation and regions come increasingly to appreciate the cultural role of cathedrals, more funding would become available at those levels'.

B4 *How in your own case was the subject matter identified and a specific brief arrived at?*

Here again the process was far from uniform. In two cases 'happenstance' and 'serendipity' were cited, while in two others the subject matter was suggested by an artist in the first instance, and in two more the Dean's decision appeared to be final, and unilateral. In three cases the donor's suggestion was predominant. With nearly half our respondents (18), however, the Chapter itself was the key player. In two cases the initiative was shared ('Chapter aspirations and donor's enthusiasms' and 'Friends and Chapter suggest') but for the remainder (14) 'Chapter discussion was invariably the starting point, usually generated from within' (13) ('Chapter agrees subject matter and brief. Anyone may propose a subject') but in one case 'Chapter responded to a proposal put to it from outside ... a working group was formed, chaired by the Dean'. Reported motivations varied from the utilitarian ('need – two altar frontals'), the architectural context ('long experience of the place, its shortcomings, needs and opportunities') to the missionary ('to make the Cathedral speak of the Christian Faith, and to interpret it to the world'), the theologically explicit ('to enhance the visibility of the role of women in the history of our salvation') and, in one case, the primarily aesthetic ('public acclaim of a piece exhibited in the Cathedral').

The procedures followed were largely similar, if not identical. They usually involved an already formalized process ('Ideas for commissions are brought to Chapter, briefs are then written by Chapter and approved by the FAC, and wherever appropriate by the Cathedrals Fabric Commission for England') and in the majority of cases (10), although not in the one just cited, the artist, architect or craftsman was directly involved as well. In one case an 'Art Advisory Group' – independent of the Chapter – was formed, while in another the essential permutation was between 'donor, artist and cathedral'. In a third case an 'independent consultant' was added to the existing framework of Chapter, Friends and FAC.

B5 *What selection procedures did you adopt in the commissioning process?*

B6 *What preliminary consultations took place, formally and informally, locally and nationally, prior to the commissioning process?*

Responses to these questions are best analysed together, largely in reverse order. Preliminary consultations were wide and variegated. Chapters consulted extensively with the FAC (12), the CFCE (8) and in nine cases with both. Significant additions at this stage were local authorities (especially planning departments – now a statutory requirement) (6), regional arts bodies (4), local educational institutions (3) and galleries (3). Although four respondents referred to 'informal surroundings' and 'recommendations within a wide pattern of contacts', one Chapter reported 'Chapter discussion only', and ACE itself was only once consulted (see D4 below for further material on ACE's role). The selection procedure itself showed similar variegation. In the minority of cases (7) informal procedures – 'consulting the Crafts Council index' (1) or 'contacting local artists/craftsmen' (3) or 'an open-ended talk with the Dean' (3) – were used. In slightly more cases (9) some kind of competitive element was involved – from artists submitting photographs and drawings (4) to a full-blown presentation before Chapter and/or FAC (3). At times the selection process was relatively exacting. In one case, 'we invited (and paid) a number of contemporary artists to submit maquettes and then invited the FAC to vote on them before the Chapter made the final decision'. In another 'The Working Group accepted a 'long list'; it reduced it first to twelve, and then to a short-list of four, from which it chose the artist after a process of discussion with each artist on site and then in an individual interview.' However, several respondents (3) were largely antipathetic to such procedures. 'Commissioning', as one put it, 'has happened through consultation rather than selection', while another favoured 'artists already known to the Cathedral'.

B8 *What part did (a) your own past experience or (b) that of colleagues in other cathedrals play in your decision making?*

It is worth incorporating the replies to this question here. While respondents divided approximately between those (14) who claimed to take both (a) and (b) into account, and those (16) who relied primarily on their own experience (either collectively or individually), only four spoke of an exclusive reliance on the experience of other Cathedrals. Several underlined their ultimate autonomy in such matters ('we refer to both, but try not to be limited by either', 'we have not gone out of our way to consult other Cathedrals in commissioning works', 'It is quite difficult to transfer experience if we are not dealing with like for like'). One respondent regarded 'theological concerns and the artistic integrity of the artist' as equally important here as (a) or (b) above.

B9 *Have there been conflicts and compromises that you especially remember?*

Unsurprisingly perhaps, given the broad-based, even eclectic, nature of the commissioning process already outlined, respondents reported the presence (12) and absence (13) of conflict and compromise in almost equal measure. Grounds for the former were relatively minor, and often highly specific ('the Bishop was furious because he wanted to influence the decision'; 'the Cathedral has been left sculpture after a six month temporary display and the sculptor has failed to collect or remove it' or 'an artist started work on a piece before being given to go-ahead'). Occasionally (3) more substantial conflicts of interest were reported. One such turned on 'competing needs for limited space within the Cathedral', two others involved archaeological considerations ('often a hazard') and a third because 'it has been difficult to convince our regular worshipping congregation that a radical option is worthy of consideration'. Sometimes (4) purely aesthetic considerations were involved ('a nave altar where the symbolism was getting too 'new age'', 'there was a lot of argument (creative) with CFCE over the treatment of garments for the sculpture') while in one case 'the figure of St X and the figure of Christ in Majesty both raised some fairly acute historical/biblical/theological queries'. But in general, although one respondent recalled how 'two dreadful conflicts preceded my own time: pre 1990', most tensions appear to have been relatively low key – 'no more' as one respondent remarked 'than is usual in any other creative endeavour'.

B7 *In your own case were the primary constraints on commissioning architectural, liturgical or financial (please be as specific as you can)?*

The final question under B is examined here slightly out of numerical order. Although five respondents answered, in effect, 'all three', and one other offered the telling riposte 'architectural/liturgical [constraints] are opportunities, financial is a constraint!', four placed liturgical constraints first ('we are looking for things that would enhance and enrich worship'), and 15 regarded architectural considerations as critical ('our cathedral is small, so new things need to be fitted into the tightest space' and 'finding what fits our building' are typical responses here). Overwhelmingly, and unsurprisingly, 23 respondents placed financial considerations first, claiming little or no money being available, or citing other, more pressing demands upon already limited resources. Nonetheless five respondents, not all from ancient or from well-endowed establishments, did not consider financial constraints as uppermost at all.

Section C Outcomes

This section of the enquiry is more overtly quantitative than the previous sections, and is treated accordingly, with minimal supporting quotation save where relevant.

C1 *Please describe local responses to your initiatives among*

a) Clergy

Positive	17
Mixed (eg 'appreciative but questioning')	8
Low key	4
Indifferent	2
Negative	1
Don't know	2
Unanswered	7

b) Congregations

Supportive/enthusiastic	10
Mixed	7
Negative/hostile	2
Unanswered	19

c)	Visitors	
	Enthusiastic	12
	Positive	4
	Interested	2
	Negative	2
	Unanswered	21
d)	Media	
	Encouraging	13
	Broadly supportive	2
	Mixed	2
	Indifferent	2
	Negative	1
	Don't know	3
	Unanswered	18

Comment

Although the non-response rate was rather high, the clergy and visitors provided slightly more positive responses to the art they encountered than congregations as such. The media emerged as more immediately supportive than might have been anticipated, with the local media perceived more positively than their national colleagues.

C2 *Were there any other specific 'spin-offs' such as postcards or posters or publications?*

Yes (postcards/posters)	21
Yes (publications)	2
No	8
No, not yet	2
Unanswered	10

Comment

Although more than half of our 41 respondents replied 'yes' their commitment to 'spin-offs' was often patchy and perfunctory. Some major cathedrals failed to publicize their artworks at all while other smaller (and sometimes more impoverished) establishments took great care to produce cards and posters.

C3 *Was there any discernible response to your initiative among artists – either locally or nationally?*

Yes (nationally)	2
Yes (locally)	20
No (nationally)	8
No (locally)	1
Not yet (unspecified)	3
Don't know	2
Unanswered	5

C4 *Has your initiative led to specific links with local and regional educational establishments (universities, colleges, schools of art, schools, etc)?*

Yes	16
Existing links strengthened	4
Not yet	2
No	11
Unanswered	8

Comment

In four cases, schools of art were mentioned, and in three others universities. In one case links with schools were strengthened, but not with the local university.

C5 *Was any Artist-in-Residence Scheme actively considered by the Chapter?*

Already established	6
Planned	2
Begun but discontinued	2
10 day Festival residence only	1
Artist on site but not strictly in residence	1
No	14
Not contemplated at present	5
Unanswered	10

Comment

Although four Chapters had well-established schemes in place, the heavy incidence of 'no' or 'not contemplated at present' was largely accounted for by lack of financial resources.

Section D Structures of Support

This section is designed to supplement the enquiries already contained in Section B. A wide variety of identified sources and structures, and the perceived role of FACs and ACE in this process are evaluated. D1–3 are presented quantitatively, with supplementary comments. D4 received more qualitative treatment.

D1 *In your experience what sources of support for commissioning and exhibiting the visual arts in your Cathedral have proved most valuable within the Chapter and beyond it?*

Friends	6
National/Regional Arts Bodies	6
FAC	5
Chapter	5
Trusts	4
Single benefactor	4
CFCE	2
Dean/Provost	2
Cathedral architect	1
Informal cathedral	1
Network ACE + FAC	1
Corporate sponsorship	1
Crafts Council	1
Congregation	1
Personal contacts	1
Local art gallery	1
Local college of art	1
Local council	1
Desire to educate	1
Ethnic awareness	2
Unanswered	5

Comment

It is clear from this wide-ranging list (where responses (47) outnumber respondents (41)) that sources of support are very diffuse. To some extent this is explicable in terms of local traditions, needs and ecclesiology. It is also clear that no fewer than ten leading sources of support were identified by an average of about 15% of respondents and that below this such sources are highly specific and largely local.

D2 *Should future support for similar projects to be primarily 'in house' or sought externally, and from whom?*

'In house'	12
Externally	9
Both	6
Depends on the commission	1
Don't know	4
Unanswered	9

Comment

The 'balance' is slightly in favour of 'in house' support, although one respondent argued that 'moral' support should be internal and financial suggest external, and another defined 'external' as 'essentially Regional Arts Boards and major charitable trusts.' A third confessed 'don't know', adding that 'we would welcome advice on this'.

D3 *Is a Fabric Advisory Committee already operative? How effective is it?*

Yes, operative	35
Inoperative	4
Effective	35
Partially effective	2
Not effective	1
Unanswered	3

Comment

The figures speak for themselves and most respondents spoke in highly appreciative terms ('has some very able experts on whom we can draw', 'very helpful with advice and suggestions', 'we try to work with them'), pointing, in three cases, to its statutory role, and, in one other case, seeing its function as 'to judge what Chapter proposes'. Criticisms were that its 'influence on commissioning can be mixed' and that it could sometimes be 'effective but not proactive'. In general terms, however, the FAC was highly valued by most of our respondents.

D4 *What specific help could ACE itself provide for you, now and in the future?*

Approximately 15% of our respondents saw three major roles for ACE – 'communicating other initiatives' (6), 'providing a pool/network of appropriate artists' (5) and 'providing information about commissioning bodies and commissioning practices'. Others (5) saw several secondary ones – 'education about wider Christian artworks (not just for Cathedrals)', 'providing, through your bulletin, publicity for our own projects' and 'identifying sources of funding'. One respondent hoped that ACE 'might directly commission art itself'. Yet although one respondent saw ACE as 'very helpful already' and another saw its 'principal task' as standing 'at the interface between the artistic world and the theological world and to discover and discern the common ground', there was an equal degree of uncertainty about ACE's precise role. Confronted by our question, one respondent replied 'none', four others 'don't know', another asked 'what are you offering?' and a seventh suggested that 'more information about ACE is needed'. Others asked 'isn't the CFCE turned to first?' and 'doesn't it duplicate the FAC/CFCE process, especially as CCC is now working with these?' Such questions clearly suggest that one of ACE's primary, and on-going activities may be to inform our Cathedral Chapters not only about the visual arts but equally about its own identity, resources and purposes.

2

Four case studies

Both the completed and returned questionnaires and our field visits to select cathedrals produced strong evidence of widely variegated provenance, patronage and policies concerning contemporary artworks. We have chosen four contrasting examples of this.

Ely

Here, to commemorate the new millennium, the Friends of Ely Cathedral gave a total of £50,000 for the commissioning of a new piece of visual art for the cathedral. The objectives were relatively clear. 'It seems to us', wrote the then sub-Dean, 'that all art commissioned in the cathedral should combine aesthetic merit with clear theological symbolism', and the commission itself was to be essentially site-specific. More explicitly envisaged was 'a relief/sculpture in any medium to go on the wall of the north-west transept. This was a very large, high, blank space (currently plastered) in the shape of a gothic arch and framed by stone. The space is 5·5 metres wide at its base by 15·5 metres high. This area is one of the first places visitors see when entering the cathedral from the main west door. It receives some direct natural light and is a space uncluttered in terms of nearby decoration, colour and texture'.

The most unusual aspect of the commission was the process by which it was produced (a detailed account is given in J Begbie (ed) *Sounding the Depths* SCM 2002, Chapters 11–13). The Friends decided to commission the work in partnership with the then Cambridge University based project *Theology Through the Arts.* It was intended that the final artwork should emerge 'from a process of exploration and discussion between the artist, a professional theologian, a representative of the chapter and of the Friends of the Cathedral. This', as the initial brief to artists made clear, 'is not about commissioning a piece of art by committee: it is a joint enquiry which is designed to fuel a creative response from each member. Ideally the process generates not only a piece of visual art but also supporting educational and theological resources'. Indeed the collaborative, cross-disciplinary aspects of the process were identified from the very beginning of the project and reflected in the three leading questions to which the final four short-listed artists were invited to address themselves on paper and at interview. These were:

A What interests you about this commission ?

B How would you approach doing justice to both the theological and artistic strands of this project ?

C How do you see this commission enhancing/complementing the development of your own work ?

The responses to these were variegated, fascinating, and sometimes contradictory. To the first question (A), for one artist it was 'the collaborative nature of the project, leading into uncharted territory that interests me most', while for another 'the meeting of the theologian with the artist would be a rich and fruitful one ... where the result is not a committee-designed hybrid but a true act of mutual understanding'. For the two other artists a more pragmatic aesthetic was paramount: 'the chance to sight (sic) a major work in what is arguably one of the most beautiful cathedrals in England' and ' a rare opportunity for me to create a permanent work that will have a long-standing relationship with the future of the building'.

To the second question (B), artists again ranged from overt thematic specificity ('the approach that I would use initially at Ely would .... be a variation of one of the many traditional themes – Crucifixion, Annunciation, Crown of Thorns, a Trinity etc' or 'I would seek to find a subject that has an established line of thought in the Church and yet is sufficiently open-ended to be interpreted in the light of contemporary culture – themes like Jacob's ladder, the burning bush, or the ascent of the risen Christ' to more general recognition that 'the discussion of the theological implications of the work comes before the completed piece and will indeed influence its development' and that 'art and theology as disciplines have a potential openness and visionary power'.

The third question (C) invoked some highly personal responses: 'I am interested', wrote one artist, 'in how to make sacred art for a new generation. The commission would be a tangible and practical opportunity to find a new way to approach this', while another acknowledged, 'I have concentrated on unravelling possible meaning through the handling of materials and refuse to separate concept from object and vice versa. This commission will enhance my understanding of my practice'.

On this evidence it is clear that the four short-listed artists wholly met the formal selection criteria, and especially expectations of 'a generosity of spirit when it comes to dialogue and communication' and 'an enthusiasm for finding new models by which we can do theology through different art forms'. Hence the final choice of artist cannot have been easy. Indeed what is especially interesting, if not necessarily surprising, was the final choice of Jonathan Clarke ('I'm no intellectual. Most of my work is produced from gut reactions, heartfelt desires or my observation of human weaknesses') by a selection committee whose outlook was itself aesthetically and theologically engaged. 'When Jonathan appeared before the committee', one member later recalled, 'he had a very grand portfolio in a black folder on the back of which, on the back cover even, was a doodle which bears a striking resemblance to the (eventual) sculpture. It was that doodle which in the end convinced the committee that he was the man for the job'. For his part the artist himself regarded it from the first as no more than a doodle and did not expect anyone to take it seriously; but, he recalls with great frankness, 'the Dean 'cooed' over it in the interview, so I realised before we started working in the 'pod' group that this was the sort of thing they were after'.

Yet despite the apparent consensus over both the choice of artist and the form of the artwork itself, the timeframe from selection to final installation was nearly two years (a year longer than initially projected). The reasons are complex, although from the fullish account given in Begbie (*op.cit.*), it may be that there was an over-calibrated commitment to 'process' during this period, involving extended 'conversations' within and beyond the core 'pod' group itself, as well as unanticipated changes of thought and its artistic expression on the part of the chosen artist himself. More precisely, at a mid-December 1999 meeting of the group 'Jonathan arrived', a memorandum records, 'having developed serious technical and aesthetic misgivings over the design that had previously attracted consensus' while 'the rest of us had arrived still enthusiastic about the previous 'agreed' design and expecting to see progress in that direction .... The rest of us did not necessarily need to come to share Jonathan's judgement ... but we did need to catch up with him before we could move on and be of much use to a new project'. Eventually – after a year – the positions of both artist and 'pod' group were to re-converge around the simplicity of the original doodle, now titled The Way of Life. If the dynamics of 'process' were unduly protracted and perhaps needlessly self-aware, the final outcome was, at least visually, successful. Both process and outcome underline what Alistair McFadyen – the theologian of the group – identifies as the basic feature of both. 'Conversation didn't appear to be an inhibition to the process of creativity but a part of it' and in this instance 'visual art of the kind that Jonathan produces works largely by indirection, by suggestion, by not making the message absolutely clear and in a sense not deciding at the outset that there IS one message'. This perhaps is the ultimate implication of our Ely case study.

Rochester

The presence of 'contemporary' art – albeit highly traditional in design and execution – in Rochester's predominantly Norman cathedral is the direct result of interaction between an Anglican Dean, a Russian Orthodox painter, and local Masonic patronage.

The artwork itself is located on the large East wall of the North nave transept, where the font is to be re-located to 'the altar position' in order to create a Baptistry. It consists of a fresco on baptismal themes – the baptism of Our Lord and St Augustine baptizing King Ethelbert and his Kentish subjects – painted by Sergei Fyodorov. The fresco is the first in an English cathedral for over eight hundred years.

From its inception the project was decanally driven. The then Dean (now retired) saw it as essentially as 'an awe-inspiring adjunct to the rites of Christian initiation …. located where baptisms and confirmations and re-affirmation of baptismal promises take place …. and intended to emphasise that adult baptism is the norm of Christian initiation'. As seen by schoolchildren and visitors it was also intended to serve both as a visual aid and non-verbal tool of mission.

In contrast to Ely for example, the Chapter agreed that 'the artist should not be faced by a committee' and 'as regards the content of the fresco he talks to the Dean alone'. Indeed, as the latter reminds us, the lower part of the fresco (the Baptism of Kent) 'was, I suspect, the inspiration of the present writer'. It is clear that the Dean, perhaps with Walter Hussey as his role model, was personally and hyperactively involved from the very outset. He took six months sabbatical as early as 1996 'to work up a scheme', which involved extended discussions with, among others, the Surveyor to the Fabric and the FAC. The latter, we are told, 'initially wanted something that was reversible'. The Dean also made good use of the extensive Romanian contacts he made while he was one of the Archbishop's Counsellors on Foreign Relations between 1965 and 1979. Indeed he came perilously close to approaching Vasile Buzolei, who had 'post 1989, painted a mural (fresco?) on the Fall of Communism in the Patriarchia in Bucharest'. Happily Canon Keith Walker, then Canon of Winchester, introduced him to Sergei Fyodorov, who was already working in England, and who had hitherto painted the frescoes of the restored Danilov Monastery in Moscow. At this point, the Dean confesses, 'although I had read his *Images or Idols?* in August 1996, I had avoided Keith Walker because I feared he would push me in the direction of some of the (to me) incomprehensible illustrations found in his book (I was, of course, totally wrong). I thus turned', he recalls, 'to the Byzantine tradition which was extant and could be said to have continued uninterrupted, whereas Reformation iconoclasm and Puritan whitewash had caused a rupture in a tradition, remains of which linked Rochester to Canterbury, to Winchester, to Sicily, to Constantinople etc'. Hence '… in my thinking and in early conversations with Sergei, we saw ourselves as reintroducing to English cathedrals an art form which had been lost. We were working within a tradition of Church art'.

Such a traditional approach to a cathedral artwork (one is tempted to describe it as 'backwards to the future'!) is, in one sense, reflected in the provenance of its funding. For, as the Dean tells us, 'the Friends of Rochester Cathedral declined to support the project, despite the Chairman's keen support'. The latter, however, also 'turned out to hold Grand Provincial Rank and persuaded the two Kent Masonic Provinces to fund a fresco to mark the beginning of the third Christian millennium …. Subsequently they have also picked up the 'on costs', caused by prolonged delay in preparing and re-rendering the surface'. Just as well perhaps that there is in fact a long tradition of Masonic patronage at Rochester, where, we were told, 'statues and glass and practice rooms for choristers are provided from this source'.

The artist himself was in residence (with accommodation, studio, preparation of the surface and provision of materials the responsibility, not of the Dean, but of the Chapter Clerk) and his work ran nearly four years late. One difficulty was strictly technical, in that the surface of the fresco wall and the correct mixture of plaster took longer than anticipated to prepare. The second was primarily behavioural, even psychological; it was that the artist himself, a distinguished icon painter – used to working in relative seclusion – found that both concentration and creativity were disrupted by the noise and bustle of the cathedral. 'He had not', he reportedly commented, 'reckoned on the difference between painting in an empty building – as he had on his last big fresco project – and painting in a working English cathedral where music and schoolchildren are part of its daily life'. Hence the artist preferred evening work, when the building was more tranquil, but his working hours were significantly reduced. As a Chapter spokesman told a visiting London journalist, 'We admit that the Cathedral initially failed to grasp the scale of the project', although he declined to comment on its overall cost to the Freemasons of Kent.

The combination, at Rochester, of decanal vision, lay generosity and artistic sensibilities – with its echoes of the Quattrocento and St Matthew's Northampton under Hussey – is a very long-standing, traditional template for locating art in sacred spaces. Whether it is, aesthetically and ecclesiologically, the most appropriate model for our own times, is perhaps more open to question.

Liverpool

Liverpool's Anglican cathedral was commenced in 1904, consecrated twenty years later and finally completed in 1978. It stands, literally and symbolically, a powerful presence in the city and its immediate hinterland. It also contains some significant, high quality, contemporary artwork – including Elisabeth Frink's *Risen Christ* outside and works by Craigie Aitchison, Christopher LeBrun and Adrian Wiszniewski within.

What is also self-evident is that despite very scarce resources for it, the Chapter's collective approach to visual art is very precisely articulated, not merely as a component of mission and ministry but through a theologically explicit sense of the cathedral's creative and prophetic role in what the present Dean sees as 'forming a relationship between the total community and Almighty God'. Unsurprising, therefore, that the most recently revised edition (2002) of the Chapter's Statement on 'Mission and Ministry' contains an explicit intention 'to build on our existing commitment to artistic creativity as a means of evangelism and a route to human understanding' (p 10). For Liverpool this entails developing both a proactive and reactive response to the arts – asking, in the present Dean's phrase, 'what can culture offer this cathedral and this cathedral offer culture?', within a wider, post-Tillichian, debate on the relationship of Theology to Culture. Indeed, it is the acting out of this debate (spearheaded by a Dean whose specialist interests include Tillich) in the Liverpool context which informs the Chapter's approach to the arts in general and the visual arts in particular.

Such an approach is clearly reflected in Liverpool's response to our written questionnaire. For them 'the motivation for commissioning works of art must be to do with the presentation of the truth claims of Christianity, in terms/forms/media that engage with contemporary, lasting (not ephemeral) culture, both local and universal, and to attract and challenge enquirers/tourists, who have no active church allegiance or religious convictions or practice'. Yet parallel to this is an equally strong sense of explicit contexts for specific works of art within a cathedral which was itself built to be, in form and totality, a work of art in itself. Indeed there is a strong assumption that works of art subsequently commissioned are expected to 'speak in their own right within the spaces provided by the cathedral'. In this sense discrete motivations, if not values, operate in differing parts of the building. Hence it is worth citing the Chapter's own account of these processes. 'In the Chapter House … the effect of the Aitchison Calvary is to offset the previously dominant motifs … by a theme of central significance. This work successfully re-focuses worship away from the Masonic and the Ecclesiastical to the Cross. In the Choir Stalls the paintings provide an in-depth pictorial presentation of the parables which complements the offices spoken and sung within this space. In the Nave the paintings present a 'reality challenge' in the context of all the imaginative symbols of corporate worship. In the Lady Chapel the Della Robbia Madonna and Child present a focus for devotion alongside similar motifs on the Reredos… In all cases the motivation is to invite people to contemplation'.

Such clarity in conception, location and execution is matched by a realistic appraisal of the likely sources of patronage. 'We have', writes the Dean, 'no wealthy/influential patron ready to think/act/initiate/enable art as a patron of the arts in Liverpool Cathedral. The re-creation of a culture in which such a person might emerge could be an important step in the creation of an atmosphere in which people expected and looked for creative artwork in a cathedral, and felt less antagonistic and sceptical about such works of art when they do appear, seemingly un-announced to the local populace, appear in the cathedral. At present', he concludes, 'I doubt whether the traditional 'Patron of the Arts', who will see it as his/her role to promote Art in a public space, is likely to emerge, at least in respect of Liverpool. But you never know'. These sentences were written before both the Cathedral's English Heritage grant of £83,000 was awarded for structural repairs (bringing the total amount given to Liverpool in the last thirteen years to £379,306) and the city's recently lauded designation as European Capital of Culture for 2008. The latter, especially, may activate one or more individuals (21st century successors to William Roscoe – Victorian Liverpool's self-styled 'Medici'!) who may – despite the pressing pastoral needs of a largely recessive local economy – see the visual arts as equally central to the Cathedral's ministry and mission, and be prepared to exercise patronage accordingly. Meanwhile the cathedral's controlling vision of its continuing, open engagement with the world of art and culture on behalf of the wider Church and in furtherance of Christian witness remains, on present evidence, miraculously, if precariously intact.

Leicester

Leicester cathedral was created from the existing parish church of St Martin in 1927. It is essentially a 'civic' cathedral in at least two senses. One is that it is physically located close to the Guildhall at the heart of Leicester's historic city centre. The other is that it retains a very strong sense of its emblematic and pastoral role in ministering to the city's political and civic elites. Indeed its South aisle was originally the Chantry Chapel of the powerful and prosperous Guild of Corpus Christi, while St George's Chapel is a major, and moving, memorial to the Leicestershire Regiment. Such a 'civic' context as this is not necessarily conducive to the commissioning and presence of contemporary artworks in the cathedral itself. Three other factors also serve to constrain the development of a more proactive agenda. One, self-evidently, is the fact that, as a Chapter spokesman put it to us, 'although this is quite a rich city, we have no money'. Another is that a major strand in Leicester's own self-image is that of being manifestly a multi-cultural, multi-faith community with an especially strong Hindu, Sikh and Muslim presence in local affairs and local identity. Thirdly, with a relatively small Chapter, discussion of, and initiatives towards, aesthetic issues is, as one member put it, 'low key most of the time'. Responsibility for all the arts lies largely, if not quite exclusively, in the hands of the Precentor, for whom the cathedral architect and the FAC have proved 'the most significant and almost sole source of support'.

Yet in such an ostensibly unpromising context for art, the Chapter continues to acknowledge both 'the need to beautify a building with recent artwork of merit in order to enhance prayer and cathedral visiting experience' and 'the need to develop educational work with art which stimulates prayer and reflection on the Judaeo-Christian story'. Hence several parallel, but interconnected, strategies are currently being pursued. One – the least exalted but possibly most effective – is the Cathedral's willingness to stage *in situ* a number of exhibitions by mainly local artists. These range from 'an exhibition of line drawings … of every parish church in the Diocese' to a valedictory show of the work of John Finnie, the Cathedral's recently retired Artist-in-Residence. Of more long-term significance was the potentially productive partnership with local educational institutions exemplified by 'a series of banners depicting the events of the Passion by a student at De Montfort University' and, more significantly still, the Cathedral's role in staging an exhibition of student work from a local Community College which had recently been re-designated an Arts College. These conscious efforts by the Chapter (and especially the Precentor) to lock the cathedral more securely (if only as exhibition space initially) into appropriate secular networks and institutions (most conspicuously the annual Castle Park Festival in August 'celebrating Leicester's history and culture past and present') are unlikely to elicit major artworks or commissions. Nonetheless they continue to affirm, albeit modestly, the links between the cathedral's religious and cultural identity.

More crucial perhaps, because of its funding potential, is the Chapter's conscious strategy of aligning the Cathedral to EMCC, the East Midlands Cultural Consortium – a Government initiative designed 'radically to rethink and acknowledge the important role of culture at regional level'. Although its definition of 'culture' is far removed from either Eliot or Niebuhr, and its ethos avowedly secular ('to recognise culture as a means to empower people and promote social and economic well-being') the Cathedral is nonetheless perceived among the quango's members as at least one among many of the region's cultural resources. That, perhaps, is something to build an art policy upon.

One other initiative remains to be identified. It is that two former Anglican churches in Leicester have become the property of the Orthodox Church and both have been adapted for Orthodox worship. Hence, as the Canon Chancellor puts it, 'Orthodox Christians are not just far away; they are here at home'. And in the Cathedral itself, in St Dunstan's Chapel, is what the visitor leaflet calls 'our wonderful icon of the Virgin and Child'. Painted in the Cretan style by the Athenian icon-painter Costas Zouvelos in 1995, and formally blessed by Bishop Kallistos of Diokelia on 2nd February 1997, it is clearly one of the Cathedral's few major artworks. It is accompanied by an excellent booklet written by the Canon Chancellor and published by the Chapter. This provides a short, accessible, commentary on the potential value and use of icons within Anglicanism as a whole and in the Cathedral in particular. It stresses the role of Leicester's 'Hodegitria' ('she who shows the way') icon as 'an image of what the Incarnation means, namely the birth of Jesus who is the word of God from his Mother Mary' (p.13). At the time of our visit a card of the icon was not yet available for purchase.

Overall the artwork installed in the last ten years has been characteristically modest – a set of engraved entrance doors, an icon, a set of bronze votive candle bowls, with a stained glass window and a set of gates for the new Visitor Centre (itself a major architectural project) currently in progress. Such items reflect the low-key, relatively utilitarian and aesthetically muted contemporary work to be found at Leicester. It is a typical example of a Chapter working with very limited available resources, and without – as yet – any significant sources of patronage within or outside the cathedral community. Whether an alternative future for the cathedral's art best lies with a closer and more high-profile alignment with EMCC and other – essentially secular – cultural consortia, even if at the expense of a more overtly Christian identity, remains, at the time of writing, an open and intriguing question.

Conclusion

These four case studies reflect the vividly contrasting motives, processes and outcomes which accompany the creation and location of contemporary artworks in our cathedrals today. At Ely consultation was, in both senses, an 'academic' exercise while at Rochester the initiative was primarily, indeed exclusively, the Dean's own. At Leicester, however, the process involved a secular consortium and interdependence with several secular, municipal and educational bodies, while at Liverpool art's place in an emergent 'theology of community' was clearly perceived and articulated by Dean and Chapter alike. Each case study reflects the sheer specificity and diversity of the local pre-conditions for the presence – and absence – of contemporary artwork in 21st century cathedrals. Indeed the highly variegated values, motives and practices recorded here mirror a similar pattern in every Chapter which responded to our initial enquiry. It is a theme to which we return in our concluding chapter.

3

Commissions in process

Works of art situated in places of worship can helpfully be located at the various stages of a process. Thus the commissioned work is approached; received; incorporated; but then sometimes neglected, ageing and removed. These several stages of a new artwork's history are traced in the following four sections.

Approached

The approach to the commission arises from a variety of locations and initiatives, ranging from serendipity to inspiration to careful study. At the serendipitous end of this spectrum is Alfredo Roldan's *Madonna and Child* in the Lady Chapel of St Bartholomew the Great, Smithfield, London EC1. Martin Dudley, the Rector, passed a West End Gallery and saw through the window an exhibition of this Spanish artist's work – still life and figurative, but not of religious subject matter. Instinctively drawn to the images, he began negotiations with the artist's gallery agent which were to issue in a commissioned altarpiece dedicated in 1999.

It was an inspired eye that led to the specially sensitive siting in 1998 of *Pietà* by Glynn Williams (Head of Sculpture at the Royal College of Art) in the Crypt of Worcester Cathedral. Bob Jeffery, then Dean, saw that in this location's forest of load-bearing columns the rendering of Mary supporting her burden – her upper torso poignantly abstracted – would be particularly telling, and so it is.

Neither of these examples can be called casual, for the clerics in question were theologically and ministerially open to the art option, prepared for surprise. The more careful, step-by-step approach may involve consultation and study, perhaps with the decision to hold a competition to choose the artist. The competition route is sometimes followed to give a veneer of democracy to the choosing process, but it can be taken only when funds adequate for the regional, national or international search envisaged are in place. Competitions, like awards, draw the attention of the art world, and may also attract the attention and support of bodies who like to see the Church projecting a bold and well thought out plan. Such was the experience of St Nicholas Cathedral, Newcastle-upon-Tyne and its competition announced in 1994. The ensuing procedure (over 500 enquiries, over 100 full applications, shortlisting, design discussion, fundraising, preparation of site) resulted in the Administrative Chapter's invitation to celebrate in their 'official welcoming' (see below) of *Eucharist* by the sculptor Stephen Cox in 1997. The procedures followed at Newcastle deserve to be known widely: the theological views of the Chapter were serially made known to the artist; the difficulty of reconciling the logistical problems of the calendar of meetings for Chapter members and for an artist of international stature (with concurrent commissions to fulfil) was surmounted, but not without much forbearance on both sides. A substantial grant from the Arts Council of England by means of the National Lottery was added to the proceeds of the sale of the two paintings by Tintoretto which had previously hung in the chosen site (see below). The financial planning therefore engaged with the arts world, ensuring proper recognition for the resulting work of art. Tim Llewellyn, Director of the Henry Moore Foundation, gave a substantial address at the welcoming.

A less ambitious competition was used in the commissioning of the work with which Ely Cathedral chose to mark the new millennium. Here the Chapter entrusted the lion's share of the commissioning work to *Theology through the Arts*. The process[1] brought together a textually focussed academic theologian with the chosen artist, together with a member of the Friends of the Cathedral (who funded the work) and a member of the Chapter who has a special interest in art and sacred space. As with many an event in church life, the pressure of deadline and the rather over-heated nature of the discussion meetings (somewhat less thrilling, it seems, for the artist than for the theologians), insulated as they were from the realities of the art world and its histories, made for an outcome lacking in conviction. *The Way of Life* (2000) by Jonathan Clarke could have benefited from some stern art criticism at the early drawing stage, together with some art historical study of the projected subject matter. Able help from the institutions of art was available had more serious study been made of what was a vastly important architectural opportunity. The scholarship of art and architecture and that of theology failed here to interact sufficiently. Perhaps this result was inherent in the initial approach plan and its scheduled completion date.

Shortened preparation may also account for the accomplished sculpture of a young woman with golden hair now in Ely's Lady Chapel. Placed high up in the window space, presumably as protection against defacement, it can be properly seen only by entering the sanctuary and looking steeply upwards for a viewing necessarily distorted. Against the glaring window's plain glass it can only be studied in outline. David Wynne's sculpture is awkward in its present siting and scale. Perhaps it will be moved around. It does have to be said that the period towards the end of a Dean's tenure of office is sometimes critically hazardous for commissions. The zeal of the new Dean may lead to art risks too; one of Hussey's successors at Chichester Cathedral was once heard speaking of its 'completion' where its art contents were concerned.

On a happier note there are examples of Chapter members engaging openly with resourceful art institutions while not selling down the river the precious deposit of theology and architecture they guard. Walter Hussey's well thought out bearing in his encounters with Henry Moore – 'not too impertinent, not too timid' – is worth weighing.

So Lincoln consulted early with the Royal Academy's Edwin Austin Abbey Trust Fund for Murals in Great Britain and received Duncan Grant's Chantry frescoes (1958) along with the co-operative guidance of the experienced Fund Secretary, who was not slow to abort a commission if he saw client or artist not playing fair. Lincoln's example of engagement with the Trust was followed by Manchester Cathedral's with murals by Carel Weight (1963), and by other places of worship.

Other commissions have been expertly steered by an experienced agent employed by a Chapter all too grateful to be relieved of the responsibility. Relieved, that is, until the agent's contract ends, and the Chapter finds itself with the care of serious and perhaps powerful works at whose birth it can hardly be said to have attended. Such works then lack and await ownership or adoption (see below).

At this all important approach stage the bold (if painful and risking of adverse criticism) decision to abort a scheme that is not progressing as hoped is wise. So St Paul's Cathedral, sensing that its research into a new baptistery was not progressing as hoped, has instead creatively designated for art the east end of the south choir aisle. As at Ely Lady Chapel the window above this site makes for poor visibility other than close to, but this bold start of an experimental nature has been made, with the display for a limited period of Sergei Chepik's *Golgotha* (1995–96). Such a site for periodically displayed images is likely to give a valuable example to other places of worship, and indeed other church premises too. Here is a meeting of the Orthodox use of icons for successive seasons and festivals with the need of congregations to experience the variety of approaches to divinity in today's art. It is all too easily forgotten how much artists themselves benefit from such showing of their work, and from the comment and criticism elicited. Chapters are rightly wary, however, of applications to show within their buildings work lacking in argued and serious sensitivity to the functions of the context. This is by no means to turn away artists who are young or little known. Choice of artists should be compared with choice of preachers and teachers: perhaps even greater care is required in the case of artists, if their contribution is to be noted by the greater number. As custodian of art and architecture the Chapter enables communication quite as much and to quite as many outside the liturgy as within.

Finally, as centres of learning, Cathedrals need access to updated booklists and references to articles concerned with the matters touched on here. With this resource they will be ready to do a service to those in their diocese and regions as well as in the wider Church who are becoming alert to the place of art in faith communities. Cathedral Chapter members need no reminding that the spaces they care for are of regional, national, international importance.

Received

The Roldan family members occupied the front rows, some travelling beyond the Spanish border for the first time, and many moved to tears by the beauty and solemnity of the occasion. In the presence of the Spanish ambassador, the Bishop of London was dedicating the new *Madonna and Child* in the Lady Chapel of St Bartholomew the Great. The reception and welcome of the newly commissioned work may well be for the artist, as for others, a moment to be treasured.

Has the artist been humanly, decently, graciously treated during the months preceding? Here the Cathedrals like Durham and Gloucester with mature, well-run artist residencies over recent years have much experience which others would benefit from. Has the cash factor been dealt with promptly and as arranged? Is a press release, with images of the work and of the work *in situ*, available in advance?

The help needed by the Chapter as the reception of the work is arrived at is no less great than at the inception of its planning. Once again Hussey's example calls out for a hearing, and for translating freshly into each Cathedral's new situation. With Hussey it was the parish church in question, of which he was (like his father before him) Vicar, but his example is not beneath any Cathedral Chapter's study. Faced with the uphill task of introducing a Henry Moore sculpture in 1944 to the parish and to the Church, he enlisted three able champions of differing ages to address differing audiences. The oldest, sixty at the time, was Bishop George Bell. In art he was patron, writer, broadcaster and scholar – and to many artists their priest. Then fifty, Eric Newton was the second, himself an artist and a critic with gifts much in demand in Britain and the United States. The third, at forty years of age, was Kenneth Clark, Director of the National Gallery and Surveyor of the King's Pictures, a communicator *sans pareil*, having an exceedingly wide grasp of art. And each of the three spoke, taught, advocated, rebutted as Hussey hoped and as need required. And plenty of need did require. This kind of seriousness Hussey took with him on to Chichester deserves great attention.[2]

From the Chapter's viewpoint, however, the new work's installation is often seen and felt to be the conclusion of their own commissioning process, which may well have entailed some painful learning experiences, quite apart from the fundraising. Needless to say, the welcome and reception of the work are, for its viewers, however, a new beginning.

This new beginning will have been sensed in numerous, small but influential ways by the people of Lichfield Cathedral when the 1991 Silver Collection was completed, bringing in the work of a team of top quality silversmiths. They produced choristers' badges; alms dish and offertory salvers; lavabo bowl and jug; flagons, chalices and patens; wafer boxes and pyx; processional cross and tapers, and a St Chad loving cup. Help and encouragement came from the Royal Academy of Arts, the Worshipful Company of Goldsmiths and a host of donors. Other commissions have in mind a wide and more diffuse reception for the new work of art: Elisabeth Frink's *Risen Christ* (1994) facing welcomingly across the city of Liverpool is an example of sculpture directed outwards from the building, as opposed to the meditative, inward intention of Chester's *The Water of Life* sculpture by Stephen Broadbent (1994).

The limitations on what, with however successful interpretation and teaching, can in fact be welcomed and received is for Chapter's wisdom and tact to judge. The daring policy of Fr Friedhelm Mennekes SJ in his Kunst-Station Sankt Peter in Cologne city centre engages fearlessly with today's major artists in the use of the church.[3] This example, in all its heroic generosity, cannot be translated easily into an English Dean and Chapter situation. A city centre Guild church in Britain might possibly take up the challenge successfully, thereby giving to cutting edge artists some of the real liturgical welcome that Art in Sacred Places (formerly Art 2000) is attempting to offer. This body has recently brought to places of worship the opportunity of showing a variety of works curated by hired professionals with a contract of limited duration. While the experience is for the church concerned enlightening, when well received and welcomed along the lines indicated above, there is the danger of missed opportunity if the welcome is skimped or perfunctory. The valuable experiment that Art in Sacred Places is conducting calls for careful monitoring if its various projects are to benefit the Church, as they well can.[4]

A different model of welcome is afforded by Art & Christianity Enquiry (ACE). The task of the ACE Loans to Churches officer is to bring artist and worshipping community into encounter, in order that any resulting loan may be arranged on as wide as possible a base of understanding. Part of the welcome given to artists may well be extended to works done in or for the Christian tradition but not necessarily situated in a place of Christian worship. Chagall, Epstein and Feibusch, for instance, brought new vigour into religious art, and the Christian community has benefited. Just as the contribution of certain theologians is brought into the life of the Church, so that of these artists – just to name a few of the Jewish ones alone – can profitably be an enrichment to theology and to Church life. Such a presentation of the images of recent artists' work in the area of faith rarely fails to stimulate understanding and questioning. Some Chapters contemplating a commission have instigated just such learning opportunities. The 'Presence' exhibitions of 2004 have been a case in point.

The welcome accorded to the incoming work of art needs to involve as broad a spread of the receiving community's life as possible. The input of a visiting art historian is greatly enhanced if, instead of being given a chilly 'expert' label, it is buttressed by a contribution from liturgy, church history, theology, prayer. This way the new work in all its initial strangeness can become a friend, a blessing, even a loving judgement in the life of the place.

Incorporated

As well as being welcomed and received by the congregation occupying the same space as their new work of art, incorporation by wider constituencies too is due to a work of importance.

For want of planning this further stage of the commission, it is all too easy to be wrong-footed by the Press. To take an example, the curators of *The Journey* exhibition at Lincoln Cathedral in 1990 could have been drawn in earlier on the furore concerning Leonard McComb's *Portrait of a Young Man Standing* (1963–83). Or they could even have stimulated it on their own terms. That particular exhibition benefited, as did the *Images of Christ* exhibition at Northampton and then St Paul's Cathedral 1993, from the services of a professional curator, who from the start entered in on planning in conversation with the Church officials responsible.

When cathedrals enter the world of art it is vital to be aware of its structures. The Church has more friends among art's dealers, critics, historians and other scholars, writers, broadcasters and columnists than it realises. It surely does the Church good if its creativity can be considered and taken up in secular and scholarly circles.

The successes in this area are all too rare. In publications about European post-war church building, the only British parish church to receive general praise is St Paul, Bow Common (Maguire & Murray 1956-1960), although the special case of Coventry Cathedral was well reported in the sixties. As is fitting, the ecclesiastical factor is published in the listings and catalogues of eg Cox, Chagall, Feibusch, Frink, Gill, Gormley, Hepworth, Kennington, Moore, Peace, Piper, Reyntiens, Sutherland, Underwood, Viola. We would have included Spencer had not his *Crucifixion* (1958) now been removed from Aldenham School Chapel (see below). But how many such publications have originated from or been authored or published by ecclesiastics? For a serious and sustained treatment from a theologically informed base of a Christian work of visual art in Britain there is only Michael Sadgrove's *A Picture of Faith* (Kevin Mayhew 1995): this remarkable account of Sutherland's Coventry tapestry deserves to be better known. Any future edition could balance the autobiographical factor with a bit more art history. At the time of writing, this moderately priced book, though still in print, was not on sale at the Cathedral. And a plea: could a reference copy – chained perhaps – of the much more expensive, superb *Coventry Cathedral: Art and Architecture in Post-War Britain* (1996) by Louise Campbell be made available in the building for consultation by visitors, worshippers and pilgrims with an interest in its art?

Specially pleasing in this incorporating stage of a commission is an article like Stephen Bann's 'The Return of the Prodigal Son' (Liverpool Cathedral 1996) in *Jahresring 43, Jahrbuch für moderne Kunst* 1997, and the essays in the same author's *The Sculpture of Stephen Cox* (1995). This kind of exchange of ideas beyond ecclesiastical structures can serve to remind cathedrals of their high place in today's national life and culture. If they are keen, as some are, to gather the views of visitors and passers by (and to make occasional selective use of them), then the opinions and considered appraisals of those whose professional lives are led close to art (whether teachers, writers, critics, historians, administrators, or dealers) are surely to be sought out as well. There would be surprises both for Church and for art if a national map of cathedrals and church resources, networks and facilities were laid over one showing educational resources of the practice and the history of art, its galleries, studios, libraries and auction houses. Here is a fruitful line of future development. Conversation between dioceses and their regional offices of Arts Council England would be a natural starting point.

Neglected, ageing and removed

This last section addresses the time factor, generally of some personal concern to Chapter members who serve only 'for the time being', and maybe in a succession of centuries. In this longer perspective the best care and study of existing religious art is clearly undertaken by national and other galleries and collectors around the world. In practical terms, if an altar, say, is to receive a new reredos, the old one (if a mural) may simply be painted over or hidden behind a new panel painting. A displaced panel painting can be re-located either within the building or outside. In periods of creativity the displaced art (architectural, sculptural, painted) may need to be preserved. Hence the diocesan museums in Continental Europe. Thus the newly restored and enlarged *Opera del Duomo* at the rear of Florence Cathedral has over the centuries come to acquire major works in their own right and of their own period which needed to be removed from the Cathedral. Few British Cathedrals have the desire, the will or the space to pursue this path with works of art that are falling into neglect or that 'belong to another century.' As in other theologico-aesthetic areas the advice of Fabric Advisory Committees is enlarging beneficially the discussion that must attend these difficult questions. In these and other areas the ministry of the American art historian Professor Monsignor Timothy Verdon, Canon of Florence Cathedral, is to be commended to English Cathedral Chapters.

In a shorter timescale, artists whose work has been commissioned for a particular place should at least as a courtesy be consulted if any variation to the original agreement is envisaged. Not to do so is to risk alienating potential donors, and among part-donors at least should be included those many artists who lower their fees for Church work. Again, the sale of the work of modern British artists for places of worship does damage to the chances of finding generous donors: two examples, one large and one small – Stanley Spencer's Aldenham School *Crucifixion* (1958) sold in 1991, and Ben Nicholson's Offertory Box (c.1930) for Rock, Northumberland sold in 2002. On the other hand Sherborne Abbey's major replacement of Victorian glass in 1995 with John Hayward's fine new window was accomplished to critical enthusiasm.

Two further time-related questions are relevant in this section concerned with change, experimentation and renewal. First is the temporary hanging of one or more works so as to interact with the liturgy or life of the congregation for an agreed season or period. This is in an old Christian tradition: the seasonal icons of the Orthodox have been mentioned, but other such visual presences as crosses and banners carried in procession, Gospel book covers, tapestries, Exultet rolls and vestments and textiles should be remembered as well. This placing of a chosen image or images at or near a regularly used altar (not necessarily the principal one) is for all concerned a very different matter from an exhibition of artwork at some site in the building unrelated to its round of worship and service. Scale and lighting and other factors will affect choices, but it may be recorded that one London church found a regularly used altar to be transfigured during successive Lents by these generous loans: *Crucifixion* (1920s) by William Roberts (Methodist Collection) and *Peter's Betrayal* (1957) by Mary Potter (private collection), and on another occasion Oliver Barratt's large, steel, walk-in sculpture *Harbour* (1994), to the mutual enhancement of the piece and of the site.

The second reflection is occasioned by the huge success of a particular work of art in its new genre: Bill Viola's *The Messenger* video, shown at Durham Cathedral's West door (1996), was seen in the baptismal context of the Cathedral's vast font, thereby yet further intensifying its protagonist's repeated submergings and re-surfacings. By nature repeatable and with scale adjustable, it was later shown also in the nave of the Anglican Cathedral in Liverpool and in St Paul's Cathedral in London, to acclaim.

It remains to praise the Methodist Church Collection of Modern Christian Art (begun in the sixties).[5] Formed by purchases at studios, galleries and sales, the collection continues to be developed as it approaches its fifth decade of travelling to city, college, church and other locations, usually accompanied by workshops and lectures. There are many for whom pictures from this collection of modern British painting have been their first experience of the possibility of a contemporary religious art, and of its integration into prayer, worship and church life. This successful and welcome initiative deserves imaginative support. The Collection's planned exhibiting could be accompanied in a given location by a curated supplementary loan exhibition of works from an ecumenical spread of owners in that location, region, diocese.

A final category of artwork or furnishing needs to be noted – place-related as well as time-related. We refer to the transfer to a new site made for the sake of continuity. Thus an existing stained glass window may sometimes be incorporated in a new church as witness to the continuity of the new building with its predecessor – the same pictured saint being patron of the new as of the old. A more venerable example of the same apostolic principle at work is the black Tournai marble font of the 1140s in Lincoln Cathedral, which was transferred (with the bowl split in transit) from a Romanesque Cathedral in Belgium. Artefacts can embody and set forth dearly held beliefs and loyalties no less potently than do words, music, gestures and architecture.

The process noted above in its various phases is used against the background of the oft remarked increasingly visual culture of today. If this is one good reason for expending care and energy, for being proactive and not reactive only, in the encounter area of Church and Theology with visual arts, the other is surely the glorious deposit within art's history of the Christian presence awaiting appropriation and study.

Notes

1 Carefully described in Jeremy Begbie (ed) *Sounding the Depths*, SCM 2002.

2 Such study begins with Walter Hussey, *Patron of Art: The Revival of a Great Tradition among Modern Artists*, Weidenfeld & Nicolson 1985.

3 See for example the exhibition catalogue (in German and English) Claudia von Blücher & Kurt Danch (eds) *Anish Kapoor*, Kunst-station Sankt Peter Köln 1996.

4 See Art 2000, *Projects in Sacred Places*, Artwise Curators, London 2001.

5 See *Catalogue of the Methodist Church Collection of Modern Christian Art*, Roger Wollen, Trustees of the Methodist Collection of Modern Christian Art 2003.

4

Mark Cazalet

An artist's view of the cathedral commissioning experience

I have worked with four buildings of cathedral status in the past four years, and in retrospect each presented a radically different commissioning experience. I believe that the success of major ecclesiastical artworks is contingent on the commissioning process employed and the support offered to the artist throughout. I would like to reflect on six areas that have conditioned the outcome of my involvement at Worcester; Manchester; Wesley's Chapel, London; and Chelmsford.

1 Statements of significance and need

The Church of England's faculty jurisdiction rules ask parishes to provide a document which sets out the reason why it is considered that the needs of a parish cannot be met without making changes to the church building and the reason why the changes are necessary to assist the church in its worship and mission. This rather stern obligation has the real benefit of focusing minds on the role of the proposed art work in terms of the architecture, existing artefacts, mission and worship. This jurisdiction does not, however, apply to cathedrals which fall outside the Faculty Law and DAC structure. Cathedrals do have Fabric Advisory Committees but their role is ultimately only an advisory one. A Dean is effectively in sole control of the Cathedral in his/her care with the cathedral Chapter as consultative parties. I would suggest a similar document is drawn up, to ensure that the initial stage of commissioning begins with reflection on what already exists and why and for whom the changes are being made. I would enthusiastically welcome the adoption of statements of significance and need as a template for the autonomous cathedral structure. It could prevent some of the compromises and misunderstandings which hinder the artist's vision developing smoothly.

2 The Brief

A The Worcester Millennium window had a short clear brief which indicated: the importance of the Garth behind the window and the neighbouring cloister windows, the subject (2000 years of Christian history in Worcester), and the option of the artist being the designer and maker, or assisting in the making by employing a glass fabricator.

B The situation at Manchester was different, with the Cathedral architect outlining a list of the elements comprising the subject and supplying a schematic drawing of their representation. No theological interpretation was made, bar the stipulation that the reredos triptych should be of the Trinity flanked by St George and St Denys, who should be situated in contemporary Manchester scenes. The stained glass panel above should depict the Paraclete. The cathedral architect's written brief was considerably redefined verbally by all four members of the Dean and Chapter and each from his own perspective. The Canon Theologian supplied the quotation: 'from the sewers of Manchester pure gold flows', contextualising the Trinity in the Booth Clibborn/Faith in the City mode of Christian socialism. The Archdeacon pointed to the thrusting new Manchester as the second national wealth producer to London, a prosperous, future-confident metropolis. The Dean did not greatly inform the brief except in linking the new buildings of the immediate area (Visitor Centre, Museum, Shopping complex) to the Fraser chapel re-ordering. I produced two written versions of the commission in order to clarify the complexity of opinions as discussions evolved. However, this lack of exact ownership of the project led, in my view, eventually to a weakened solution, which I regret.

C Wesley's Chapel was a good example of an open brief formed in co-operation with Leslie Griffiths, now Lord Griffiths, the Superintendent Minister. It was conceived as a memorial window for Donald English, a much-loved past World Methodist Council President. Leslie intimated that a second window could follow to balance the first, also commemorating 20th century doctors of the Methodist church. We walked around the building making an inventory of the existing iconography, artefacts and hierarchy of spaces. We agreed the need for an accessible, democratically figurative style which would employ biblical narrative in a contemporary manner. The briefing discussions included important introductions to Methodism's distinct sense of liturgy, via Wesley's dictum of a simple thing done well. It was accepted that I draw up my own written brief on the basis of our conversations which included an analysis of the site.

D Chelmsford offers another paradigm of briefing whereby ten minutes after arriving I was met by the Dean in the nave and asked what subject the site suggested to me. I made an intuitive response, and serendipitously proposed the single image – he had been considering, the tree of life. This was a happy but rather terrifying resolution to the briefing process. My portfolio contains a considerable body of tree works which supplied a great deal of pre-prepared reference material as both visual and theoretical underpinning. I wrote a briefing statement which included an analysis of the site.

3 Funding

A The Worcester funding was handled deftly, with the Dean's assurance that there was a sufficiency. Actually he was sheltering me from the very real fund-raising that had to take place on the back of my initial designs, and continued till after the installation. The Dean was intent on the window being financed solely by a millennium subscription.

B The Manchester funds were a secured figure but, whereas the Dean told me that should my design require more all I had to do was ask, the architect was emphatic that I understood that no further funds would be forthcoming. The stained glass far exceeded the original remit, and was therefore made at cost price. My budget came from an undisclosed total sum for the chapel refurbishment which included the architect's works.

C Wesley's Chapel started with a small percentage safe, but the greater part to raise during the manufacturing process, the last tranche pledged at the inauguration itself.

D Chelmsford were nudged into making a county council grant application from an ecology fund. This grant should have paid for the entirety but, as we progressed through the grant giving stages, the total award slipped to a third of the original figure. After a lunch with the cathedral's key benefactor full support was secured.

4 The selection process

A Worcester requested slide presentation packs from a number of artists before deciding to interview two. We were both invited to visit the site and make a formal presentation before a panel made up of members of the Dean and Chapter, and FAC. The only hitch in an otherwise flawless arrangement was the procedure of a preliminary session of questions from both candidates simultaneously, which invited a degree of jockeying. The advantage of the FAC's involvement in the appointment procedure was to establish a broad level of responsibility in the appointment, and perhaps better fund-raising opportunities.

B Manchester received my name as a recommendation, and what I supposed to be only an initial visit was actually, as it quickly became apparent, an interview with the Canon Theologian, joined by the Dean, and later in the day separate talks with the Precentor and the Archdeacon. When the initial conversation ended much theology, history and sociological insight had been communicated along with the commission.

C Wesley's Chapel, I believe, looked at a range of artists before I met Leslie and talked informally; there was a committee formed but their role seemed perfunctory.

D Chelmsford was another instance of being nominated as a recommendation.

5 Design stages

For all the commissions undertaken, and for many not won, I produce a site analysis paper. This attempts to summarise the opportunities, issues and problems of the intended works. Usually this is followed by discussion, and leads to a preliminary design. The initial design is a hard thing to quantify. It acts as the touch paper to the full-scale work, showing clearly the motifs, handling of the medium, sensibility of expressiveness, and ultimately is a visual contract. But it must not become a definitive interpretation. There needs to be room for growth in the production of the actual work. The risk that fires creative engagement would be lost if the process ends in a merely technical scaling up exercise after FAC approval. Showing the design is a highly charged event, not least as patrons seem highly reluctant to agree to a design fee, despite the process being inevitably front loaded in research time. Only two clients agreed to a specified payment at the design stage.

A Worcester dealt with swathes of history that were wholly unfamiliar, requiring considerable research and consensus finding in the final selection of subjects. The Canon Librarian put me in touch with an eminent county historian, local newspaper archive, and informed city figures. Three weeks was spent drawing at sites in the county and city, another week went into reading accounts of the lives depicted. During this period I stayed in the cathedral close with the Canon's family, which provided an excellent background to the clergy and congregational mixture. The initial design was a $\frac{1}{20}$ schematic rendering of the basic flow of the compositional forces and the hierarchy of subject placements. This was agreed informally by the Dean and Canon Mackenzie, and a full size acrylic painting followed. This was then presented to the Dean and Chapter, and the Cathedral architect. One Canon disliked the Catholic emphasis of several of the chosen individuals (Mary breastfeeding Christ, the martyrdom of St John Wall, and Dame Laurentia MacLaughlin) and the allegedly marginal Anglicanism of the two clerics (Richard Baxter and Studdert Kennedy). He was given a fair hearing but had to rush to another appointment abruptly, whereupon the design was unanimously passed. The FAC met in camera and passed the design with two letters of concern, which I replied to but got no return from. The Dean made it plain that they were not going to stand in the way whatever they concluded. Etched and engraved glass was a new medium to me then, so a full-scale trial window was made. This was a crushing disaster with the figures only half the proportion needed, and far too indistinct in their paleness. The absolute support of the Dean and Chapter (bar one) and the can-do mentality of my fabricators were the enabling power behind the successful outcome.

B The Manchester brief required scenes of the city as backdrops to the action of the iconographic subject. This required drawing the city for a week in consultation with Canon Atherton, who was keen to show me the third of the community disenfranchised by the more obvious property development and retail booms. The initial design was approved by the Dean and Chapter, except for theological unease in the original brief of the Paraclete (in the stained glass window) flying over the Trinity in the reredos. The result was the compromise of the bird remaining, but partially abstracted, representative of Noah's dove or more generally an image of ascent. The final design was again seen and commented on individually. The new bird was a hit with the clergy but not with the architect. The reredos seemed to satisfy the disparate requirements made, but only with the Archdeacon's stipulations that all faces were smiling, Marks & Spencer's name was removed in case of offence, all references to Sales were removed, and that the busy bargain-hunting crowds bustling in the opposite direction past St Denys became sedate shoppers. I would now like to repaint all four recantations, and feel it was cowardice not to have argued my case. That, however, was the price of a unanimous verdict prior to the FAC meeting. The FAC approved both elements of design with one dissenting suggestion that people come to church for nice comforting experiences.

C Wesley's Chapel. Had a low-key presentation of the initial design, with only one request from a member of the panel that his likeness be removed from the image. The full-scale design was accepted without alteration.

D At Chelmsford the Dean introduced me to the advisory committee in order to float the proposed mural project. This was endorsed, and the design process sanctioned. The Dean accepted the finished design without alteration. With some excitement it was also shown to the particular patron of the cathedral, and a group of volunteers who were all enthusiastic. The Chapter were not shown the design. The next presentation was to the FAC, accompanied by a second statement to broaden out the references, particularly to Judas hanging in the branches and the ecological aspects of the image. The County Council were also invited to a presentation in due course.

6 Reception of the work

A At Worcester there was a grand candlelight Millennium service. In a frosting of snow a beautiful liturgy of light was conducted by the Bishop, concluding around the window in the garth. I was overwhelmed, and felt the window had truly become part of the building and its community. I have returned to run a sixth form art day around the commission, and have led two groups to speak in front of it. The Dean organised an open talk on the themes and process of the window, which filled the chapter house. Apart from one Colonel Blimp who objected to nose picking being depicted (and he yielded to a public show of hands by those who had never picked their noses) all went well.

B Manchester laid on a good service complete with the director of music playing my favourite Messiaen organ work. The Archdeacon's address warned people not to judge a new artwork on first appearances but to give it time, even if it seems strange at first. The Dean said that media coverage was not a good idea as the black St George was likely to provoke vandalism if reproduced in the newspapers. The Precentor, I was told, does not like it and the other clergy like different parts; the architect said I could not be surprised at a mixed reaction if St George was depicted as a black man! The choristers did respond well, exploring the surface and finding some of the hidden elements, and began to relate to them.

C Wesley's Chapel held a large service which was positive and the window has led me deeper into Methodist ties which have been a great source of enrichment.

D The Chelmsford mural, the latest to be dedicated, drew these words from the Dean in the course of his address:

> This great Tree of Life expresses the ancient ideas of the beginnings of Creation in Genesis – and the apocalyptic vision at the end of all things, with the Tree of Life standing in the city of God with leaves for the healing of the nations. But it also invites all of us to act – to save this tree – to find ways of living which are sustainable, where we live in harmony with the very things we depend on for our survival. Like the warning canaries in the coalmines this is a majestic warning symbol we cannot ignore.

5

Ways forward: conclusions and recommendations

This enquiry has attempted to explore, from a variety of perspectives – from the theological to the sociological, and from the institutional to that of the individual artist – recent and current Dean and Chapter policies with regard to the commissioning and display of works of art in England's cathedrals. It became clear that, not unlike the latters' own architectural development, there is not always a common pattern in their patronage, provision or policies. Nor is there yet any ecclesiastical equivalent of the Arts Council, whether located in Church House, the Council for the Care of Churches, or in the dioceses themselves. Unsurprisingly, therefore, much artistic endeavour in cathedral settings, while often of high quality, is essentially localized, eclectic and piecemeal. At the same time, paradoxically, with some contemporary evidence of cathedrals reinventing themselves (often at the expense of parish churches) both as primary foci for local worship and secular pilgrimage in a supposedly post-religious culture, the pre-conditions for both the presence and patronage of art there have never been more propitious. Yet, as our research indicated, four clearly identifiable constraints continue to operate.

One is financial. Few Chapters have deep pockets of their own with which to initiate art work, and some are still dominated by a mind-set that sees art, especially by living artists, as essentially extraneous to, rather than an integral part of the life, worship and fabric of a cathedral. For them the physical maintenance of cathedral 'plant' takes precedence over aesthetic addenda. Fewer still reported dependable sources of non-ecclesiastical patronage, either local or national, while corporate munificence of the late medieval or contemporary North American kind was relatively rare. Sometimes, too, potential funding – from whatever source – was inadequately explored, or the perceived absence of such sources was used as a rationalization for inactivity.

A second is strictly architectural. Not all cathedrals, especially internally, offer self-evident opportunities to display artworks either as freestanding art objects or as an integral component of fabric and liturgy. Some buildings simply lack suitable spaces or are already crowded with extant, well-loved, if aesthetically unsatisfactory works of art. Most are, in any case, listed buildings. Hence the impulse tends to be to retain the spatial and decorative status quo. To do otherwise, even if appropriate, requires determination, stamina, vision and leadership.

Thirdly, all too often, the lifestyles and mind-sets of both the clerical and artistic professions are mutually perceived as exclusive rather than inclusive, as parallel rather than convergent. Many artists tend to regard cathedral Chapters as unworldly, inward-looking, and cut-off from current developments in the art world, while some Chapter members, in their turn, perceive artists as gifted, bohemian and often unreliable 'outsiders' – marginal, both socially and credally, to the local Christian community. The reasons for the origins and persistence of this 'hermeneutic of suspicion' (the phrase is Paul Ricoeur's) are, of course, highly complex and embedded in the history of English culture itself. Yet its consequences, as we found on the ground, were all too often, little mutual contact between, even knowledge of, the parallel worlds of the cathedral and the artist, or between religious and educational institutions at local levels.

Finally, the role and reception of art in our cathedrals is inevitably bound up with broader questions concerning the perceived functions of 'religious' art, however defined, in a Western Europe where religious engagement and experience is increasingly personal, private and freely negotiated rather than public, communal and culturally mandated. In such a context – where Word formally maintains primacy over Image, especially within the Protestant tradition – it is not always easy for both churchmen and artists to regard art as a tool of mission or as a signal of transcendence (or both) or to regard it as axiomatic that the invisible can be made visible through an art which is not an optional extra but an essential element in the religion of the Incarnation. Furthermore, such a relatively proactive perspective is sometimes difficult to sustain, partly because, unlike the Orthodox, our theologians (especially, perhaps, our Canon Theologians!) do not feel compelled to provide the conceptual apparatus for the artist – when approaching the latter's world. More critically still, perhaps post-modernity's major impact on Christian art has been that, in Peter Fuller's phrase, 'there is now no normative iconography in the West at all, especially where the art world and the theological world are both in transition'.

Yet our own research reveals much thought and activity at local levels which belie both the pessimism and the problematics identified above. Indeed it is clear that in many places the relationship between the cathedral and the community still refracts the relationship between that community and God, and that art is often bound up with that process. How this happens is sometimes primarily through the personal activism of a Chapter member or leading layperson, through the brokerage of ACE itself, and through the growth of mutual trust, as well as shared accountability at the heart of many local Chapter initiatives. At the same time, we do not regard such a potentially optimistic scenario as necessarily permanent or failsafe. Hence in the light of this enquiry we also make the following formal recommendations:

1 That every cathedral should have a named individual, preferably at Chapter level, with specific responsibilities for the visual arts. Such a person might be called the Diocesan Visual Arts Officer. Their responsibilities should include:

1·1 liaison with ACE and Arts Council England
1·2 liaison with local art education bodies and institutions
1·3 liaison with local artists and galleries
1·4 identifying potential sources of patronage for art works
1·5 raising knowledge and awareness of the meaning and purpose of religious art within the cathedral community and beyond.

2 That an annual one-day conference of Diocesan Visual Arts Officers be established, possibly linked to the existing annual gathering of Deans of cathedrals.

3 That a joint ACE – Arts Council initiative be taken to create a Christian Arts Advisory Service (CAAS) to facilitate the commissioning process between religious bodies, artists and patrons. It could function 'on line'.

4 That the existing ACE Awards for Art and Architecture, and the ACE Loans for Churches Officer form a focus and forum for the exchange of ideas and projects relevant to cathedral settings.

5 That greater efforts be made to ensure that the visual arts become part of the core curriculum of theological education, and that a theological component be introduced at Diploma level within Colleges of Art.

6 That, while respecting local variations, certain models of 'best cathedral practice' be made more generally available by CAAS (see 3 above) for consultation by individual Chapters.

7 That the journal *Church Building: the Magazine of Ecclesiastical Design* be encouraged to place greater regular emphasis than at present on visual art as well as built forms. A discrete section of the journal could meet this need.

8 That ACE and the Arts Council should consider a joint venture publication called Seeing and Believing – a guide to visual art in English cathedrals.

Select bibliography

Jeremy Begbie (ed), *Soundings the Depths*, SCM Press 2002

Mark Cazalet & Tom Devonshire Jones, 'New religious art', *Country Life*, 17 April 2003

Tom Devonshire Jones, *New Art for Old Cathedrals*, NADFAS Review, Autumn 2003

—, (ed), *Presence: images of Christ for the third millennium*, BibleLands 2004

Ruth Gasson & Michael Winter, *A Survey of Visitors to Four English Cathedrals*, Church Study Unit 1994

Stephen Platten & Christopher Lewis, *Flagships of the Spirit: Cathedrals in Society*, Darton, Longman & Todd 1998

Keith Walker, *Images or Idols? The Place of Sacred Art in Churches today*, Canterbury Press 1996

A Future for Church Buildings, Christian Heritage Forum, Church House Publishing 2003

Art 2000: Projects in Sacred Places, Art in Sacred Places 2001

Heritage and Renewal – the Report of the Archbishops' Commission on Cathedrals, Church House Publishing 1994

To be a Pilgrim: Meeting the Needs of Visitors to Cathedrals and Churches in the United Kingdom, International Council on Monuments & Sites UK 2000

Appendix 1

English cathedrals & the visual arts Preliminary questionnaire

Please feel free to supplement your replies with any further comments, observations or addenda (eg minutes, press cuttings, correspondence, etc) that you consider relevant. Such material will, like your responses to the questionnaire, be treated as **strictly confidential**.

Response from _

of _ Cathedral

Section A Theological and Pastoral

1 How would you describe your Chapter's main motives for commissioning and or exhibiting works of art in a Cathedral setting, especially in relation to:

a) Worship _

b) Doctrine _

c) Mission _

2 If you have remained inactive in this area, please indicate any primary constraints operative in your own case.

_ _

3 How seriously does your Chapter take the relationship between religion, artworks, beliefs and experience in your own 'public space' among

a) congregations _

and (b) visitors? _

4 How do you encourage the personal input of the artist(s) involved?

_ _

Section B: The Process of Patronage

1 What, if any, have been the sources of patronage for the visual arts in your cathedral, whether

a) permanent works of art_ _

or (b) temporary exhibitions? _ _ _ _ _ _ _ _ _ _ _ _ _ _ _ _ _ _

2 Has patronage been primarily ecclesiastical or lay?

_ _

3 What forms might such sources of patronage take in future?

_ _

4 How, in your own case, was the subject matter identified and a specific brief arrived at?

_ _

5 What selection procedure did you adopt in the commissioning process ?

_ _

6 What preliminary consultations took place, formally and informally, locally and nationally, prior to the commissioning process?

_ _

7 In your own case, were the primary constraints on commissioning architectural, liturgical or financial (please be as specific as you can)?

_ _

8 What part did (a) your own past experience or (b) that of colleagues in other cathedrals play in your decision making?

_ _

9 Have there been conflicts and compromises that you especially remember?

_ _

Section C: Outcomes

1 Please describe local responses to your initiatives among:

a) Clergy _

b) Congregations ____________________________

c) Visitors ____________________________

d) The Media ____________________________

2 Were there any other specific 'spin-offs' such as postcards, posters and publications?

____

3 Was there any discernible response to your initiative among artists – either locally or nationally?

____

4 Has your initiative led to specific links with local and regional educational establishments (universities, colleges, schools of art, schools, etc)?

____

5 Was any 'Artist-in-Residence' scheme actively considered by the Chapter? With what consequences?

____

Section D: Structures of Support

1 In your experience what sources of support for commissioning and exhibiting the visual arts in your Cathedral have proved most valuable within the Chapter and beyond it.

____

2 Should future support for similar projects be primarily 'in house' or sought externally, and from whom?

____

3 Is a Fabric Advisory Committee already operative? How effective is it?

____

4 What specific help could ACE itself provide for you, now and in the future?

____

Section E Addenda

Please use the space below to include any further information, comment or reflection that you feel may be relevant to our enquiry, but which are not directly elicited by the questionnaire. Meanwhile thank you again for your help with this project.

Appendix 2

Names and addresses of organizations

1 Art & Christianity Enquiry (ACE)

Begun in 1991, ACE draws together all for whom the visual arts are vital in their understanding, teaching and practice of the faith. Now a charitable trust, it organizes lectures, undertakes research, energizes, encourages. Quarterly bulletin by subscription, complimentary copy on request.

Director Revd Tom Devonshire Jones
107 Crundale Avenue, London NW9 9PS
Tel and fax 020 8206 2253
Email enquiries@acetrust.org
www.acetrust.org

2 Art and Sacred Places (ASP)

Art and Sacred Places promotes interaction between religion and art, largely by siting specially commissioned contemporary art in sacred places. It engages new audiences, currently in the south east, by exploring the relationship between art and spirituality, encouraging debate and understanding. ASP's work is based on the conviction that art and religion share fundamental concerns and explore similar territory, albeit in significantly different ways. ASP was founded under the auspices of Bishop John Gladwin in 1999 and became a charity in 2001.

Director: Revd Keith Elford
15 Canford Drive, Addlestone, Surrey KT15 2HH
Tel and fax 01932 885137
Email keith.elford@lineone.net
www.artandsacredplaces.org

3 Association of English Cathedrals (AEC)

Established in 1990 and authorized by the Administrative Chapters of the Anglican Cathedrals as their representative organization, the AEC deals with governmental agencies, the General Synod, and their constituent bodies and the Churches' Main Committee on behalf of the English cathedrals, provided only that it cannot commit any individual cathedral chapter to a specific decision. It monitors the consequences of the Archbishops' Commission on Cathedrals. Membership consists of one representative of each Administrative Chapter.

Chairman Very Revd Christopher Lewis
Secretary Very Revd Gordon Mursell
Birmingham Cathedral, Colmore Row, Birmingham B3 2QB
Tel 0121 262 1840
Fax 0121 262 1860
Email dean@birminghamcathedral.com

4 Cathedral Administration and Finance Association (CAFA)

In 1975 cathedral administrators and treasurers began, as a body, to exchange information on all matters touching on best practice and the most effective administration of the English Anglican cathedrals. The association now enjoys a valued link with the Association of English Cathedrals for which organization it undertakes research as needed. There is an annual conference and regular regional meetings.

Chairman Mr John Roberts
Admin Secretary Mr Jamie Milford
Treasurer
Church Commissioners, 1 Millbank, London SW1P 3JZ
Tel 020 7898 1678
Email jamie.milford@c-of-e.org.uk

5 Cathedral & Church Buildings Divisional Group

The Division was formed in 2002 from the staff formerly serving the Cathedral Fabric Commission and the Council for the Care of Churches, and supporting the work of the Archbishops' Council in relation to cathedral and church buildings. The CCC is the Church's national advisory, grant-making and educational body supporting dioceses and parishes with the care, use and development of parish churches and their contents and churchyards. The CFCE is the central planning body with advisory and regulatory functions relating to the fabric, contents, setting and archaeology of the Church of England's cathedrals and their precincts. The Head of

Division is Secretary of the CCC and CFCE and also acts as the lead officer of the Church Heritage Forum (see below).

At a time of major change in ecclesiastical and secular heritage sectors, the Division is responsible for developing and maintaining relations between Church and State, national and local bodies on church buildings matters, and for the development of the Church's vision of how the Church of England may (in partnership with the State and local communities) best meet its responsibilities for its church buildings.

Overall the Church of England is responsible for 16,000 parish churches and 41 cathedrals which form the centres for the Church's worship and its mission in the community. These buildings and their contents represent 14 centuries of religious architecture, art and history, which have continuously developed up to the present day, and are still developing. Some 13,000 are listed buildings (including 35% of all the country's Grade 1 buildings), while many churchyards are an important ecological resource.

Chairman Chair of the Church Heritage Forum
Members Chair of the Cathedrals Fabric Commission; Chair of the Council for the Care of Churches; four other Members (appointed by the Appointments Committee from within the Synodical members of the CCC and CFCE)
Head of Division Ms Paula Griffiths

6 The Cathedrals Fabric Commission for England

In 1949, at the request of Deans and Chapters, the Cathedrals Advisory Committee was set up to give help and advise on places and problems affecting the fabric, furnishings, fittings and precincts of cathedrals.

In 1981 the Committee was reconstituted as a permanent Commission of the General Synod, under the title The Cathedrals Advisory Commission for England.

In 1991 the Commission was further reconstituted as a statutory body under the Care of Cathedrals Measure and renamed the Cathedrals Fabric Commission. The Commission has regulatory powers under the Measure. Before implementing proposals affecting the cathedral, its contents or its surroundings, the Dean and Chapter require the approval of the Commission in specific cases, or of a local Fabric Advisory Committee appointed jointly by the Commission and by the Dean and Chapter. It also has advisory functions relating to the architecture, archaeology, art and history of cathedrals and their precincts.

During 2003 the Commission issued guidance on the implications of the Disability Discrimination Act for cathedrals and churches.

Chairman Rt. Hon. Frank Field MP
Vice-Chairman Sir Michael Llewellyn-Smith
Head of Division Ms Paula Griffiths
Tel 020 7898 1887
Email paula.griffiths@c-of-e.org.uk
Office Church House, Great Smith Street, London SW1P 3NZ
Tel 020 7898 1866
Fax 020 7898 1881
Email general.enquiries@ccc.c-of-e.org.uk

7 The Churches Conservation Trust (formerly the Redundant Churches Fund)

The Trust was set up in 1969 to preserve churches of historic, architectural or archaeological importance which had been declared redundant and so were no longer needed for pastoral use. With over 300 churches in its care, the Trust warmly welcomes visitors and encourages educational visits. Many churches are open daily, while others have keyholders nearby. Trust churches host occasional services as well as concerts, exhibitions and lectures. The Trust, which is a registered charity, receives its statutory funding from the Church Commissioners (30%) and the Department for Culture, Media and Sport (70%).

Director Mr Crispin Truman, 1 West Smithfield, London EC1A 9EE
Tel 020 7213 0660
Fax 020 7213 0678
Email central@tcct.org.uk
Head of Conservation Miss Sarah Robinson
Head of Public Affairs Ms Constance Barrett

8 The Council for the Care of Churches

The Council for the Care of Churches (CCC) was formed in 1921 to coordinate the work of the Diocesan Advisory Committees for the Care of Churches, which advise diocesan chancellors on faculty applications, and clergy, churchwardens, architects and others responsible for church buildings and their contents on their care, use and development.

The CCC's priority is to enable parishes to release through responsible stewardship the mission and worship potential of church buildings. We seek to encourage and assist parishes in the care and conservation, use and development of the Church's buildings including their contents and churchyards.

The CCC advises the Archbishops' Council on all matters relating to the use, care and planning or design of places of worship, their cartilages and contents; acts on the Council's behalf in contacts with government departments and other bodies and in negotiations with professional bodies over church inspection and repair; and assists in the review or revision of legislation relating to church buildings and their contents.

The CCC provides Diocesan Pastoral Committees with detailed reports about the architectural and historic qualities of churches likely to be declared redundant. It also submits specialist advice to diocesan chancellors, Diocesan Advisory Committees and parishes on proposals which are or may become the subject of faculty applications, eg the construction of church extensions, re-ordering schemes, the sale of church furnishings, the partial demolition of churches, the conservation of significant furnishings, and related archaeological work.

The CCC maintains contact with Diocesan Advisory Committees through regular circulation of information, by an annual meeting for Chairmen, Secretaries and other members and by visitors. The membership of DACs is varied: it includes both clergy and lay, some with professional expertise in architecture, art history and archaeology, and others of no specialist knowledge but of sound judgement and experience, or representing the views of English Heritage, the local planning authority and the amenity societies. Every diocese has specialist advisers on organs, bells, clocks, archaeology, and so on.

The CCC administers funds (generously provided by charitable bodies) for the conservation of furnishings and works of art in churches, and collaborates closely with English Heritage, the Heritage Lottery Fund, National and other Lottery distributors and other grant-making bodies. Advice is available from the Council on specific conservation problems.

The CCC is concerned not only with the care and conservation of ancient buildings and their contents, but also with the development of places of worship and the encouragement of good new furnishings and works of art. Advice is available and parishes are encouraged to consult the Council's register of artists and craftsmen and to examine photographs of their work.

The Council's specialist committees offer expert advice on conservation matters and administer grants from charitable foundations for the care and conservation of significant or historic furnishings and works of art in churches and churchyards. Churches in England, Scotland and Wales, of any denomination, are eligible for these grants. In addition, under an agreement reached with the Wolfson Foundation, the Council consider applications for grant aid towards fabric repairs for grade I and grade II Anglican churches in England, Scotland and Wales.

Funding church repairs and applying for grants

Those seeking information on sources of funding for church repairs should contact the Council for the Care of Churches and/or the Historic Churches Preservation Trust (see Organisations section). A booklet, *Fundraising for your Church Building: A Simple Guide*, is available from Church House Bookshop (see p 38). An electronic version is also available on the Churchcare website <www.churchcare.co.uk>.

Publications

The Council has an extensive list of publications on practical and technical matters relating to the care and conservation of church buildings and their contents. A complete list of titles and prices is available on request from Church House Bookshop or from the Council's offices.

9 Deans' Conference

The Deans' Conference is the meeting together (three times annually) of those who preside over their Cathedral Chapters to reflect upon cathedral issues of particular concern to Deans in their public and cathedral roles.

Chairman The Dean of Canterbury
Treasurer The Dean of Exeter
Secretary The Dean of Carlisle,
Cathedral Office, 7 The Abbey, Carlisle CA3 8TZ

Tel 01228 548 151; 01228 523 335
Fax 01228 547 049
Email dean@carlislecathedral.org.uk

Designed by Phil Baines
Printed by SpecialBlue